Written &

Arlene Stev

Design & Illustration by Larry Kazal

QUILL • New York • 1983

Arlene Stewart and Joan Van Raalte left the glamorous
world of publishing to do first-hand
research for this book. Most of their waking hours are now
managed by their offspring. Both claim
to have a secret desire never to see a *Sesame Street*
character again.

Library of Congress Catalog Card Number: 83-60333

ISBN: 0-688-02129-8 (pbk.)

Printed in the United States of America

First Quill Edition

1 2 3 4 5 6 7 8 9 10

To our own
extremely well-behaved
babies

Annalee Stewart Levine
&
Pierson Van Raalte

Cont

Introduction

Who's Boss Now?

eNts

"Who's Boss Now?"

Dear Parents,

We don't have to tell you that this book is
about the toughest job in the world. We're parents
and we know what it is like out there on the
front lines with baby, so the least we could do was
to get a few laughs out of it. Let's face it,
when you worry about having enough *scented*
cornstarch in the house, or come to consider
shopping alone in the supermarket as "fun," things
must be getting serious. This is where
No Bad Babies comes in. Falling somewhere
between a parents' pacifier and a mother's guerilla
warfare manual, *No Bad Babies* blows the
tamper-proof lid off the sacrosanct world of babies
and reveals the humorous truth about life
with these loveable little dictators.

Written entirely without help from any medical
"authority" or baby "professional,"
No Bad Babies is designed to help parents feel
better. . . as in – "I feel better because
your mother's car just pulled out of the driveway"
. . . or "I feel better because your
father just gave Pasquale Jr. a $5,000 trust fund"
. . . or "I feel better because I found
some ear plugs that really work."

Babies, we have on good authority, are among the
world's most adorable creatures.
In fact, in a recent survey entitled "Cunning
Creatures on Land & Sea", it was
indisputably proven that babies are the cutest
group within any species.

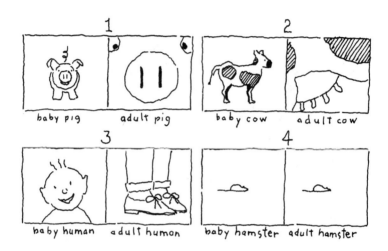

1   2

baby pig   adult pig   baby cow   adult cow

3   4

baby human   adult human   baby hamster   adult hamster

This is their greatest strength!!!!!
Babies know this and use this! Ounce for ounce, a
baby has more appeal than can
be resisted by any adult. Babies are fresh . . .
wholesome . . . charming . . . BUT
DANGEROUS! They will use their powers
everyday to get what they want—
other kids' toys, endless attention, your valuable
stereo equipment, and anything
delicate and fragile. It is only with the utmost
concentration that new parents can
keep any control over their lives
at all!

Offering absolutely no guarantees, we can
confidently say that, taken in small
doses, this book will provide relief from everyday
strife. Serious cases should try
to get in 3 or 4 pages an hour; for those who are
desperate enough to be asking
mother-in-law to help out for a week, we recommend reading this entire book
right now.

WARNING: Keep this book in a safe place.
The paper is highly absorbent.

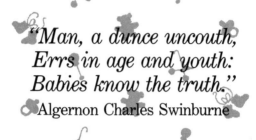

"Man, a dunce uncouth,
Errs in age and youth:
Babies know the truth."
Algernon Charles Swinburne

"I'll try anything once."
Alice Roosevelt Longworth

1
Preparing for baby

Secret Side Effects
of Pregnancy

Obstetricians and pregnancy books tell mother-to-
be all about such *common* side
effects of pregnancy as swollen ankles,
disturbed sleep, and disappearing waistlines.
But what about those other side effects –
the secret ones, the ones you never
hear about until it's too late? The editors of
No Bad Babies, in cooperation with the
Mothers of America, are ready to
go public with this long-suppressed information:

- A lack of interest in swimsuit and shoe sales
- Telephone shoulder from mother-in-law's incessant phone calls
- Bewildered exhaustion from endless advice people give you
- Broken nails from trying to open "child-proof" pre-natal vitamin bottles
- New awareness of poorly-designed chairs
- New awareness of ice cream stores. WARNING: This does not go away after baby's birth
- Writer's cramp from baby shower thank-you's
- Embarrassing knowledge of soap operas and daytime TV
- Growing awareness of bad-tempered infants in obstetrician's office
- Recipient of sympathetic looks from women
- Recipient of uneasy looks from men
- Fear of revolving doors
- Mental map of easily accessible restrooms
- Wariness of attractive girlfriends
- Fear of long lines in supermarkets
- Stubbed toes from visiting the bathroom four times each night

The Worst Baby Names in the World

The importance of the right name for baby cannot
be overstated. Would you go to
a gynecologist named Romeo? . . . or have your
taxes done by a Blondie? Let's
face it, names are where parents can really help
to make or break their baby's
chances of success.

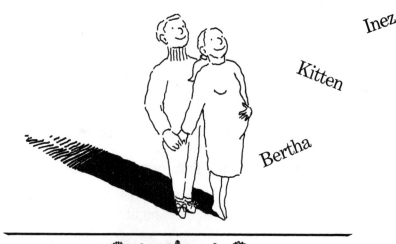

Inez

Kitten

Bertha

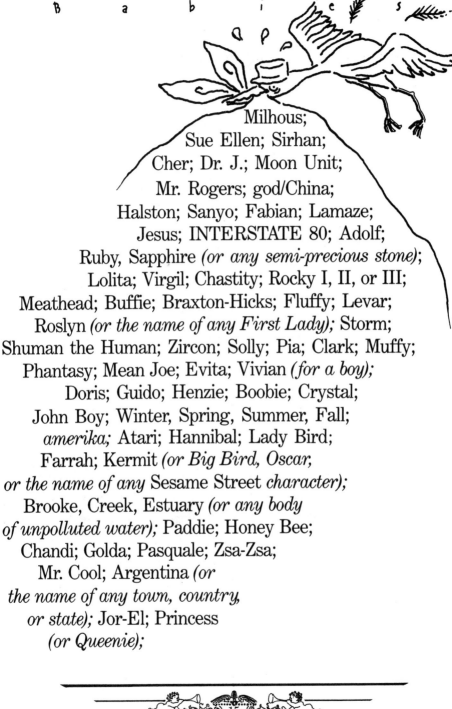

B   a   b   i   e   s

Milhous;
Sue Ellen; Sirhan;
Cher; Dr. J.; Moon Unit;
Mr. Rogers; god/China;
Halston; Sanyo; Fabian; Lamaze;
Jesus; INTERSTATE 80; Adolf;
Ruby, Sapphire *(or any semi-precious stone)*;
Lolita; Virgil; Chastity; Rocky I, II, or III;
Meathead; Buffie; Braxton-Hicks; Fluffy; Levar;
Roslyn *(or the name of any First Lady)*; Storm;
Shuman the Human; Zircon; Solly; Pia; Clark; Muffy;
Phantasy; Mean Joe; Evita; Vivian *(for a boy)*;
Doris; Guido; Henzie; Boobie; Crystal;
John Boy; Winter, Spring, Summer, Fall;
amerika; Atari; Hannibal; Lady Bird;
Farrah; Kermit *(or Big Bird, Oscar,*
or the name of any Sesame Street *character)*;
Brooke, Creek, Estuary *(or any body*
of unpolluted water); Paddie; Honey Bee;
Chandi; Golda; Pasquale; Zsa-Zsa;
Mr. Cool; Argentina *(or*
the name of any town, country,
or state); Jor-El; Princess
(or Queenie);

15

What Not to Pack in Your Lamaze Kit

Although childbirth is a well-established practice
dating back to long before the
invention of baby showers, there have always been
those people who have attempted
to refine what is essentially a one-woman
operation. Today, for instance, there
is the wide-spread influence of Fernand Lamaze,
who was inspired to bolster the fortunes of the
sagging candy industry by introducing
lollipops to the delivery room.

Through the use of lollipops and favored "focus
objects," the Lamaze Method allows
Mom (and Dad) the unique opportunity to experience childbirth without any pain-
killing drugs.* To accomplish this, however, they
must have with them a carefully-
packed "Lamaze Kit." *No Bad Babies'* experience

---

*This is not to be confused with any of the
so-called "natural" childbirths occurring before the advent of
anaesthetics.

and dozens of letters from mothers
confirm that the "right" kit should not include
any of the following:

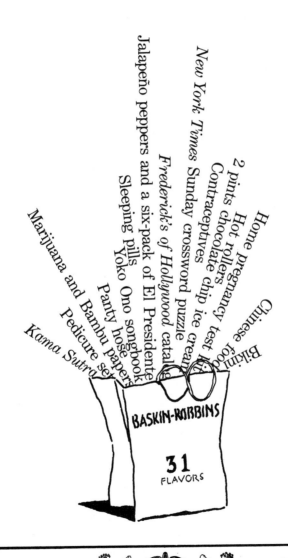

Jalapeño peppers and a six-pack of El Presidente

New York Times Sunday crossword puzzle

Frederick's of Hollywood catalog

Sleeping pills

2 pints chocolate chip ice cream

Hot rollers

Contraceptives

Home pregnancy test kit

Yoko Ono songbook

Panty hose

Marijuana and Bambu papers

Pedicure set

Kama Sutra

Chinese food

Bikini

BASKIN-ROBBINS

31 FLAVORS

Labor:
Ways to Procrastinate

There are some things in life worth
looking forward to. Labor is not one of them.
Therefore, we cannot be critical of anyone who
might want to delay this state
of affairs. Serious procrastinators will have no
trouble finding compelling reasons
not to go into labor: suppose pains start before
you have worn your most expensive
maternity outfit . . . or on the morning of
Bloomingdale's biggest sale . . .
or even three hours before J.R. and Sue Ellen are
to be re-married on *Dallas*?

Labor is not the easiest thing to
procrastinate over, it is true; but if you are "stuck"
with World Series tickets, invitations
to a chocolate tasting, or you think the signs
of the zodiac are unfavorable, you could
try to delay the inevitable by using
these methods:

...and you know how much I've been looking forward to that sale that's starting Friday at Gordon's and if I miss the James' party they'll never forgive me, after all, I really did mean to go the last 2 times and Daddy would really appreciate it if we could help him clean the garage and,

BABY ?

1. Forget to buy Jello

2. Visit a busy labor room

3. Make a date to see all your mother-in-law's friends one week after delivery

4. Suspend yourself in gravity boots

5. Babysit for any newborn baby

6. Skip your last Lamaze class

7. Disagree with your husband about the right focus objects

8. Fly backwards over the International Date Line

****
*   *
* "If men bore the children, there would be only *
*   one born in each family."   *
*   *Reflections of a Bachelor*   *
*   *
****

The 12 People a New Mother Least Wants to See

Having a baby can do wonderful things for your
soul. It does not, however, do
wonderful things for your body. It can stretch, age,
broaden, and otherwise render
you looking like something between a deflated
knackwurst and the "Before" file
at Weight Watchers.
That is why you will almost certainly require an
extended period of privacy (anywhere
from 2 days to 20 years) to get back
into shape.

During this period, your ego is very fragile. You
must be prepared for the worst.
We recommend that you take all precautions not to
admit to your house, yard, or
lobby any of the following:

Thin girlfriends

Anything weighing less than 150 pounds

Old boyfriends

Your mother-in-law's friends

Anyone with an older child

Anyone who didn't see you pregnant

Your obstetrician

Jane Fonda

The person who got your job

Richard Gere

Single women in their twenties

Your husband's co-workers

Inspired Baby Gifts

The arrival of baby immediately sends friends,
relations, and next-door neighbors
to the baby section in the department store.
Unfortunately, most baby gifts
today are so ordinary and boring, they're hardly
worth taking back. In fact, on average
parents spend more time wondering what to do
with all those acrylic hat and bootie
sets than they spend with their in-laws.

We have given this problem serious thought
and have reached the conclusion that
if you want your gifts to have any distinction at
all, you should demand that your
relations and friends give from the following list:

UNDER $5.00
- Deluxe jar of Tucks pre-moistened pads
- One gift certificate to Burger King
- One copy *No Bad Babies*

UNDER $25.00
- Case of Scotch-Guard
- Aspirin shaker
- Several copies *No Bad Babies*

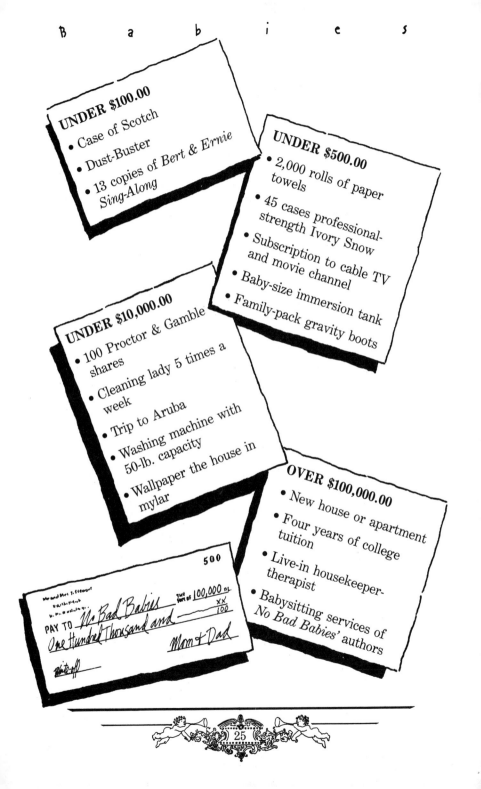

UNDER $100.00
- Case of Scotch
- Dust-Buster
- 13 copies of Bert & Ernie Sing-Along

UNDER $500.00
- 2,000 rolls of paper towels
- 45 cases professional-strength Ivory Snow
- Subscription to cable TV and movie channel
- Baby-size immersion tank
- Family-pack gravity boots

UNDER $10,000.00
- 100 Proctor & Gamble shares
- Cleaning lady 5 times a week
- Trip to Aruba
- Washing machine with 50-lb. capacity
- Wallpaper the house in mylar

OVER $100,000.00
- New house or apartment
- Four years of college tuition
- Live-in housekeeper-therapist
- Babysitting services of No Bad Babies' authors

"Parenthood remains the greatest single preserve of the amateur."
Alvin Toffler

"The reasons grandparents and grandchildren get along so well is that they have a common enemy."
Sam Levenson

2

Bringing baby Home

The Right Stuff

Competition begins in the cradle, and every
new baby needs all the help he or
she can get. To insure an easy passage into
the "real" world, *No Bad Babies*
recommends that all newborns immediately
seek out:

The Right Mom
Survival training graduate with strong back, thick
skin, developed arm muscles, and
wipe-clean surface. Oblivious of noise, stains, and
bad smells; enjoys working long
hours. Self-sacrificing, skillful diplomat with
thorough knowledge of local take-out menus.

The Right Dad
Ex-model with private income and Olympic
medal in floor gymnastics. Working
knowledge of alphabet, peek-a-boo, and toy repair.
Able to open medicine bottles in
the dark and subsist on crackers, cold pizza, and
leftover Chinese food for extended
periods of time.

The Right Aunt
Robust child psychologist, expert in pre-verbal
communication, currently researching
"The Effects of Imposing Discipline and Order
on the Under-Two's." Single, no
children; lives one block away, above fruit store.

The Right Uncle
Childless owner of toy store and tireless mimic
of Bert and Ernie, horses, dogs, and
a menagerie of other animals. Hates sports on TV;
loves zoos, circuses, theme parks,
and chocolate milkshakes. Available for walks on
weekends and at odd hours.

The Right Grandparents
Should have no other grandchildren, a summer
home in Disneyland, and an empty
beach house in Hawaii. Reluctant to spend
money on themselves, but astute
investors in stocks, securities, and long-term
tax-free bonds. Avid amateur
photographers. Live next door to Toys-R-Us.

The Right Neighbors
There are only two kinds of neighbors to have:

1. A pediatrician who enjoys working off-hours.

2. No neighbors at all.

The Right Pediatrician
Trustworthy father/mother figure
who accepts Mastercard, VISA, and American
Express . . . and your phone calls.

The Right Babysitter
Clean-living teenager of saintly disposition without
any obvious social life (has signed
up for the next six New Year's Eve's). Regards
parents' welfare in importance
as next only to baby's future and puts both far
above own interests. Cordon Bleu
baby chef; impervious to drudgery, indifferent
to income.

the 'TAN TRUM'

| DISCONTENT | AGITATION | EXTREMELY VOLATILE | MELTDOWN | |

BABY PROFILE # 27

The Preppy Baby

Birth weight: 7 lbs., same as Preston I, II, and III's
Choice of drink: very dry double apple juice
Love object: mommy's Izod appointment book
Temperament: similar to a duck decoy
Favorite toy: stuffed alligator
Preferred reading: F.A.O. Schwarz catalog
Bedtime: after *Wall Street Week*
Relationship with parents: very secure
First word: "Neat!"

Murphy's Law
for Babies

Baby will always prefer to soil an unused
diaper than one worn for two hours.

Parents' need for sleep increases as baby's
decreases.

Baby's noise level increases as
parents' favorite TV show comes on.

What can spill, will.

What can break, will.

What can stain, will.

Any cranky baby will "behave beautifully" for
grandparents.

Any ridiculous outfit given to baby will fit.

Any toy parents hate, baby will love.

Baby will always have a diaper rash or bruises
the day you visit the pediatrician.

Parents will always discover they are out of milk
after stores close.

Baby will always have on dirty clothes
when friends drop by.

Baby will always start to cry the moment you
get into bed.

Parents will not be able to remove the lid from the
last jar of baby food.

100's of New Ideas!!

No Bad Babies' Catalog of Baby Equipment That Hasn't Been Invented Yet

BABY N-R-GEE

With BABY N-R-GEE your baby can generate enough power to warm up a family meal for three. Compact unit will entertain baby for hours. Simple to install. Dull black finish.

Price range: **$3,000–4,100**

"THE HAPPY HOUR"
LIQUOR FILLED PARENTS' PACIFIER

Similar in design to baby's own, this adult model helps prevent undesirable parental rages. Useful whenever parents are tired, hungry, or unhappy. Hard plastic shield provides soothing facial exercise while preventing embarrassing dribbles. Available in Brandy, Scotch, Piña Colada, and vintage Bordeaux.

Price range: **$10–15**

MR. MAGNET TOYS-GO-HOME!

Oversize, sturdy, powerful magnet serves the dual purpose of teaching babies about magnetic fields while developing self-clean-up skills. Simply attach accessory magnets to toys and give to baby before bedtime. Comes with 1,000 magnets.

Price range: **$45–60**

HAPPIE VAC-CIE™

A light-weight push toy with special feature for parents – when the HAPPIE VAC-CIE™ is moved backward or forward a compact 25 h.p. vacuum is set into motion. Comes with pink or blue replacement bags.

Price range: **$95–110**

PARENTS-DREEM VIBRA CRIB

Lullabye and goodnight for baby. . .while you watch *M*A*S*H*. Easy-to-assemble crib eliminates need to rock baby to sleep. Comfort dial to suit baby's mood: "Dozy", "Difficult", and "Warp One". Full-length endboard discourages baby from crawling underneath and tinkering with hydraulic mechanism. Meets most safety standards. Harness optional.

Price range: **$4,500–5,200**

"TAKI-183" GRAFFITI-FREE PAINT

Developed in Communist China, this revolutionary wall-covering prevents those unsightly hard-to-remove "decorations" on walls, floors, and furniture. Spray paint, crayon, chalk, wall posters, felt markers, and grease simply will not adhere to any surface painted with *TAKI 183*. No more scraping or sandblasting. Available in "hi-tech" battleship grey only. **WARNING:** Cats, dogs, and certain other pets have been known to react adversely to *TAKI 183*. In cases of extreme hair loss, consult your local veterinarian.

Price: **$75 per gallon**

15 Things
a Baby Most Wants

We know that at an early age babies are aware
of three things: their stomachs, their
surroundings, and their power over their parents.
Some babies are content to lie
about being coo-coo'd to by adoring relatives.
Others take a more aggressive
stance and exert a hard-to-ignore influence over
their environment. But no matter
what their temperament, all babies have similar
wants. And what do they want?
No Bad Babies recently interviewed thousands of
babies age 1 week to 2½ years.
The following emerged as "highly desirable" with
this discriminating age group (smart
grandparents take note):

Year's supply of chocolate pacifiers

8-hour cassette of the
opening and closing of *Sesame Street* and *The
Muppet Show*

Subscription to
"Fruit of the Month" Club

6 sets of doting grandparents

Baby-size Mr. Rogers cardigan and sneakers

Primary-colored
army surplus helicopter cockpit

3 Moms:
1 to play with
1 to pick up and cook
1 to send out for frozen yogurt

Indoor trampoline, slide, & swing set

Year-round Christmas tree

2 Dads:
1 to "watch sports" on TV with
1 who is Fozzie the Bear

Banana plantation

All of neighbor's toys

Endless supply of shopping bags

Similac's Ice Cream Man machine

Year-round home in Disneyland

Identifying Baby Stains

What motherhood lacks in thrills, it more than makes up for in spills.

1. How to remove stains:
The proper time to deal with a stain
is the moment mother-in-law arrives.
2. Test your stain recognition:
Below are common baby/parent stains.
See how many you can identify:

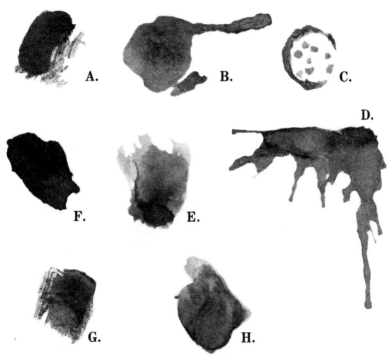

A.

B.

C.

D.

F.

E.

G.

H.

ANSWERS: A. Bananas; **B.** Diaper ointment; **C.** Vomit
or pepperoni pizza; **D.** Urine (mostly for parents of boys);
E. Beer; **F.** Fruit; **G.** Blood; **H.** Egg

BABY PROFILE # 2

The Prince and the Princess

Birth weight: no comment
Favorite food: peeled grapes
Love object: Camp Beverly Hills t-shirt;
Bloomingdale's charge card
Temperament: inner-directed
Favorite toy: Look'n See mirror
Favorite activity: being pampered
Relationship with parents: one-sided

"The best way to give advice to your children is to find out what they want and advise them to do it."
Harry S. Truman

"Cleaning your house while your children are still growing is like shovelling the walk before it stops snowing."
Phyllis Diller

3
Living with Baby

16 Saturday

Diary of a New Mother

6:15 Baby wakes. Wants favorite records.

7:45 Baby helps make breakfast...
on the carpet!!

9:20 Baby tears pages from Spock
(section on DISCIPLINE)

10:30 Baby wakes Dad.

11:15 BABY LOCKS DAD IN BATHROOM!!!
Dad climbs out window, wrenches ankle.

12:00 ~~HAIRCUT + FACIAL = CHEZ VITO~~
re-schedule

1:15 Baby loses pacifier...Dad loses ace
bandages.

2:00 Baby's Naptime
| Dad's Naptime

3:45 BABY/DAD Playtime (NFL Football, Ch. 4)

5:06 In-laws drop by to say "Hello"

7:05 call baby-sitter for Sun. nite movie

8:13 In-laws leave... baby loses pacifier

8:30 ~~BABY'S BEDTIME (wants juice)~~

8:45 ~~baby's bedtime (wants books)~~

9:03 ~~bo's bedtime (wants walk.)~~

10:21 bedtime!

Sunday 17

6:00 BABY wakes. WANTS MR. ROGERS.

7:30 MR. ROGERS NEIGHBORHOOD
(find baby's cardigan)

8:15 Baby helps make breakfast
on bed! Wakes Dad

9:21 Dad locks self in bathroom.

10:30 CHILDREN'S MUSEUM OUTING!
〜〜〜〜〜〜〜〜〜〜

Baby falls asleep

12:30 lunchtime (send Dad's shirt + pants
to cleaners A.S.A.P.!)

1:33 DAD + BABY Naptime

(Friends drop by: wake
baby)

4:15 In-Laws drop by to return pacifiers

5:05 In-Laws' friends arrive with camera!?

6:00 MOVIE   Cancel b. sitter

8:03 baby loses pacifier

8:20 baby goes to bed

9:01 In-Laws leave

43

New Mother's Stress Test

There can be no song of praise too great, no litany
of virtues too long, no homage too reverent
for today's mother. Caretaker of baby, husband,
home, relatives, friends, and careers, the
modern mom shoulders a load so broad that even
Jane Fonda had to get into shape to handle it!

But all this valor takes its toll. Sometimes we
may not be as serene as mothers are meant to be.
If you find yourself holding your breath
and counting to 10 more than twice an hour, or feel
that you passed your tether some way back, you
should take this test as soon as possible.

---

1. Do you find yourself reading
   Pat The Bunny after baby
   has gone to bed?

   a. yes

   b. no

2. Are you (a) as easily, (b) less
   easily, (c) more easily
   distracted than your baby?

   a.

   b.

   c.

   d. please repeat question

3. Do you consider taking out
   the garbage "a break"?

   a. 25% of the time

   b. 50%

   c. 75%

   d. 100%

4. When was the last time you
   said to yourself, "Maybe I'll
   stop on the way home for a
   drink"?

   a. yesterday

   b. two years ago

   c. don't understand question

5. Do you still call your single friends?

   a. yes

   b. no

6. Do you still have any single friends?

   a. yes

   b. no

7. How often does your husband accuse you of being a hypochondriac?

   a. once a day

   b. only at night

   c. never, he's too sick

8. When a friend of yours tells you she's pregnant, do you:

   a. laugh hysterically

   b. stare

   c. cross another babysitter off your list

9. How would you complete this sentence: "My mother-in-law is so unbelievable; why, last week she . . .

   a. finally went home."

   b. told my husband to get off the sofa and wash the dishes."

   c. phoned from Barbados to say she's staying on an extra week."

10. If you had to compare yourself to an animal, it would be to a:

   a. gazelle

   b. pack horse

   c. elephant seal

11. If you could change one thing about your life now, you would:

   a. get a new hairdresser

   b. spend even more time cooking and cleaning for baby

   c. spend less time awake

   d. all of the above

12. If your husband told you you were the most wonderful wife and mother in the world, would you:

a. wake up and feed baby

b. burst into tears

c. get the address of the bar he's calling from and order a cab to bring him home

13. Do you often fantasize about:

a. having a cleaning lady

b. getting more than five hours straight sleep

c. waxing your legs

14. Does Jane Fonda make you:

a. feel disgusted and annoyed

b. start exercising again towards a "new you"

c. reach for the Godiva chocolates

15. If you went on a shopping spree now, would you buy:

a. Sony Walkman

b. pair of black spike high heel shoes

c. two nursing bras

SCORING:

All "a"s – *You're okay*
All "b"s – *Get another babysitter*
All "c"s – *Get another husband*

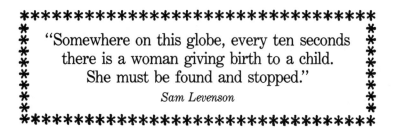

****
"Somewhere on this globe, every ten seconds
there is a woman giving birth to a child.
She must be found and stopped."
Sam Levenson
****

BABY PROFILE # 17

The Feminist

Birth weight: this side of deprived
Duration of labor: longer than any man could endure
Choice of drink: milk from "free cows"
Temperament: interventionist
Favorite toy: musical mobile that plays, "I am Woman"
Means of transportation: EPA approved stroller
Favorite activity: having diapers changed by a man, on principle
Relationship with parents: prefers to have own life
First word: "ERA"

New Father's Stress Test

The modern father is under seige. Not only is
he expected to come home after work,
but he is also expected to be a "full partner" in
raising baby – and that means
diapering, too. Many new Dads burn-out quickly
under this tremendous pressure.
The following *No Bad Babies* questionnaire has
been designed for new fathers to
help them determine if they are approaching
any dangerous stress points:

1. When your wife told you she was pregnant, did you:

   a. get out your old train set

   b. go missing for two days

   c. throw a tantrum

2. Have you resumed sexual relations since the birth of baby:

   a. yes

   b. yes, with wife

   c. no comment

3. Does the company of your wife tend to make you:

   a. hyperactive

   b. hypersensitive

   c. hyperventilate

4. Have you and your wife had an argument in public since the birth of baby:

   a. yes, it was her fault

   b. yes, it was baby's fault

   c. no, but it would have been her fault

5. Do you feel you are not getting enough attention:

  a. 90% of the time

  b. 98% of the time

  c. yes, and baby ignores me, too

6. When wife asks you to help with the housework, do you:

  a. remind her *you* worked that day

  b. take the dog for a walk

  c. play dead

7. Before the birth of baby, did you take an active interest in:

  a. international politics and current affairs

  b. wife's job

  c. sex

8. Since the birth of baby, do you take an active interest in:

  a. legal forms of sedation

  b. wife's conversation

  c. sleep

9. Do you consider Mr. Rogers:

  a. a kind-hearted counsellor and close personal friend

  b. an overpaid wimp whom wife and pediatrician like

  c. a threat to your sexuality

10. Do you get angry and irritable when:

  a. wife turns off cartoons

  b. you can't find *your* pacifier

  c. you see single men enjoying themselves

11. Which of the following do you want baby to have:

  a. your sense of humor

  b. your record collection

  c. your debts

12. If you were going to change your career, would you become:

  a. international playboy

  b. merchant marine

  c. lighthouse keeper

13. Evaluate how the following have changed since baby was born:

	a. Decreased	b. Unchanged	c. Increased
Food consumption	a	b	c
Alcohol consumption	a	b	c
Uses of uncontrolled substances	a	b	c
Use of profanity	a	b	c
Random tantrums	a	b	c
Smoking	a	b	c
Day-dreaming	a	b	c
Time "working late"	a	b	c
Time at playgrounds	a	b	c
Time awake	a	b	c
Time spending money	a	b	c
Time watching TV	a	b	c
Time taking photos	a	b	c
Time avoiding household chores	a	b	c

SCORING:

All "a"s
Micro-stress level
Congratulations, you are a "full partner" and can look Mr. Rogers in the eye.

All "b"s
Normal stress level
Could improve. You can look father-in-law in the eye.

All "c"s
Danger stress level
You should find a good doctor, a good live-in helper, and a new wife.

BABY PROFILE # 39

The Macho Baby

Birth weight: 10 lbs. 14 ozs.
Choice of drink: piña coladas
Favorite food: 2 Hungry Man frozen
TV dinners (beef)
Love object: swimsuit poster
of Christie Brinkley
Favorite TV personality: Erik Estrada
First word: "Hey, you"
Temperament: belligerent; dislikes pink

Grandma Manners

Answers Your Questions

Little Lazybones

Dear Grandma Manners,

My son Dimitri is two years old. He has no inclination to walk. Should I worry?

Stir Crazy

Dear Stir Crazy,

No. Many adults have had trouble walking ... Mickey Rivers, Dean Martin, Gerald Ford, and Sammy Davis, Jr. come to mind. Others have never had a need to walk, like Jacqueline Onassis and George Steinbrenner. Psychologists are now discovering that walking is not as important as it seems.

* * * *

Dealing with a Defect

Dear Grandma Manners,

My husband is the biggest slob in the world!!! And I'm ready to call it quits! Since the birth of our son Fabian, he's become nothing but a pig at the table! He eats with his hands slobbering food down his beard and shirt. More food goes over the people sitting near him than in his mouth! I can't take it!! I'm also concerned that he's a bad influence on Fabian.

Mrs. Pasquale Cool
New York City

Dear Mrs. Cool,

Have you thought that you might be serving your husband difficult foods? Why not try giving him bite-size dishes like Chitlins au Gratin, Raisin-Velveeta Logs, Spam Fingers Flambé, and Peanut Butter & Jelly Petits Fours. These and many other of my favorite recipes are collected in my latest book, *Grandma Manners Five-Minute Gourmet*, $16.95 plus $2.50 postage and handling.

* * * *

Bad Impression

Dear Grandma Manners,

Every time my infant son vis-

its the pediatrician he empties his bladder on the good doctor. Is it time to find a new doctor?

Humiliated

Dear Humiliated,

Certainly not. Your son's doctor should be used to this as it happens to him several times a day. That's why he wears those leather suits.

* * * *

The Bore Next Door

Dear Grandma Manners,

Is it right for a 25-month old boy to constantly scream and yell at our 20-month old daughter? We like to have our neighbor's son visit but lately between his fighting and the messiness he generates we just don't know what to do. Would it be impolite not to answer our doorbell?

Name withheld

Dear Nameless,

Your problem is more common than you think. Those people used to live next door to us.

* * * *

Dear Grandma Manners,

My husband Chip insists there is such a thing as "male lactation" and says he plans to "share the load" breastfeeding our baby.

Already, he spends too much time fussing with his clothes, wearing loose smocks around the house, and drinking milk shakes. He says he is not worried about feeding in public. What can I possibly tell my relatives?

Mrs. K. B. Czerkowitz
New York City

Dear Mrs. Czerkowitz,

You can only hope that your husband will be so tired after the delivery that his milk doesn't come in for quite some time. We applaud his helpful spirit and recommend he contact the La Leche League for more information on diet, clothes, and exercise. They will be very happy to see that your husband is helping out and will not ask you any embarrassing questions.

Contents of Refrigerator

Babies don't only change your laundry piles, but your diet too!

Before

6 trays ice cubes

Large bottle Stolichnaya

2 semi-full boxes Chipwiches

Bowl of 3-alarm chili

Prime porterhouse steak

Moldy end of Brie

Quart of half-sour pickles

Guacamole dip with fuzzy mold

2½ slices pizza "with the works"

Half-empty box After Eights

3 servings Mom's lasagna

Pre-natal vitamins

2 cans Coco Lopez

Case of Rolling Rock

Nearly-empty quart milk

Bottle of Dom Perignon for "The Big Day"

and After Baby

Your mother-in-law's frozen chicken soup
Your mother's frozen chicken soup
2 of your mother-in-law's chicken casseroles
3 of your mother's chicken pot pies
8 Hungry Man chicken dinners

Large plastic container of your
mother-in-law's chicken soup
Left-over meatloaf and instant mashed potatoes
3 open jars baby applesauce
Economy-size Velveeta cheese
6 forgotten jars assorted baby food
Half-eaten banana
Large bowl Jello with crusty top
Limp stringbeans, carrots, celery, and broccoli
Family-size Stress Tabs
Gallon of plain yogurt
Gallon of orange juice
Case of Diet Coke
Gallon of skim milk
Bottle of Dom Perignon
Low-calorie cottage cheese
Left-over Weight Watchers Fish Dinner
4 servings diet pudding
Unopened quiche from supermarket
Rotting container of diet "cream-cheese" spread

Baby myth # 1

"She'll sleep through the night now"

Next to evidence of intelligence, new parents most
anxiously await this development
in baby. That is why this comforting myth
can be used with great effect by
well-rested relatives on new parents. As sleep-
starved individuals they will grimly
clutch to any ray of hope and more than
likely reply (out of politeness),

We certainly hope so.

To which "quick-witted" visitors will add,

If not now, she should in a month or so.
It must be very hard on baby.
Do you have any Sanka?
Coffee keeps me up.

Baby myth # 2

"The second one is easier than the first."

This much repeated platitude is entirely without substantiation. The reason for its persistent popularity may be the "misery loves company" frame of mind that parents of two or more children fall into. More likely, it is due to the highly virulent strain of multiple-Grandma and Grandpa-ism that is seemingly impossible to control. It should be ignored when heard, and the potential victim should quickly make an appointment with a gynecologist for a refresher course in birth-control techniques.

Baby myth # 3

"Babies are small, helpless creatures."

Much has been made of the delicacy and
dependancy of babies. It is important
to set this matter straight right away. Long-
suppressed scientific studies have
just been released that reveal that the average
baby, on a pound-for-pound basis,
possesses a greater tensile strength than that of a
5-ton pickup. More recent findings
prove that baby's lung power, when harnessed
to an electrical feed-in, can supply
enough power to run all the food processors in
a city the size of Buffalo for one day.

Baby myth # 4

"After six months your sex life will be normal."

Actually this is true. But what your obstetrician
failed to tell you is that on the
New Parent's Sexual Frequency Chart, "normal"
falls somewhere between the level
attained by parents of six or more children and
the average resident at Leisure Village.

Average New Parents Sex Life

Before Baby   **After Baby**

TIMES PER WEEK

····Dad
---Mom

Baby myth # 5

"There is no such thing as an ugly baby!"

While this may be true from a new
parent's standpoint, the rest of the world is a little
more objective and sharp-sighted.
In fact, one of the greatest pleasures that all
parents have is comparing their
children (favorably) to other newcomers under the
guise of gushing admiration. Key
clues to their real attitude can be found in
such phrases as:

"He has your ears, doesn't he?"

*

"I don't know who she resembles more—you or
Francis the M . . . I mean her father."

"They always look so different when they get
older."

*

"That's SOME BABY!!"

Milestones in Baby's First 2 Years

Today, parents are so busy looking
for "officially sanctioned" signs of growth and
development in baby that they often
miss moments that truly deserve recognition.
Why not take a few minutes now
to think about these exciting developments
in your baby:

First Year	Second Year
MOTOR	
Sails toys in toilet	Flushes toilet
Breaks priceless heirloom	Breaks priceless heirloom deliberately
Unfolds laundry	Sends laundry out window
Learns to turn on TV	Learns to select channels
Pulls off socks	Pulls off tablecloth

LANGUAGE

Understands what parents say	Ignores what parents say
Points at objects in book	Points at objects in Childcraft catalog

SOCIAL

Laughs at Dad's jokes	Laughs at Dad
Manipulates Grandma	Manipulates you
Becomes angry with you	Becomes angry with toys
Insists on selecting favorite foods	Insists on selecting favorite restaurants
Has uncontrollable bowel movement in public	Has uncontrollable bowel movement in public

MENTAL

Imitates cat	Imitates Gary Coleman
Hides object	Searches for hidden object
Bites toy duck	Bites pediatrician
Points at own genitals	Points at stranger's genitals
Refuses to wear mittens	Refuses to wear same thing twice

SENSORY PERCEPTION

Notices colors	Notices mother's poor taste in clothes
Vomits on anyone	Vomits only on members of family

101 Uses for a Live Grandmother

Grandmothers can be a great help to new parents
in all sorts of ways. In many parts
of the world (U.S.A. excepted), Grandma is
considered to be an expert on all
things, and often a new parent will turn to her for
advice. Here at the *No Bad Babies*
Institute for Love, Peace, and Happiness, we
hate to see any talent going to
waste, and so we have compiled a comprehensive
list of the many uses for the new
grandmother. We are delighted to present
it to the new parent:

1. *to* **50.** *Babysitter*

51. *Tireless family counselor*

52. *Highly-trained dust and dirt spotter*

53. *Unpaid cleaning woman*

54. *Stain removal specialist*

55. *Phone-in doctor/diagnostician*

56. *Phone-in analyst*

57. *Amateur pharmacist*

58. *Laundry and clothes care specialist*

59. *Expert shopper*

60. *Expert at returning things to stores*

61. *Unreluctant marriage counselor*

62. *Source of good gossip*

63. *Family financial counselor*

64. *Family purchase advisor*

65. *Fortune teller/career advisor*

66. *Baby birthday party organizer*

67. to **70.** *Cordon Bleu holiday chef*

71. *Colorful family historian*

72. *Patient nursery rhyme reciter*

73. *Amusing storyteller*

74. *Endless toy buyer*

75. *Bathroom hygienist*

76. *Relentless insect killer*

77. *Provider of all sizes of plastic bags*

78. *Provider of groceries in emergencies*

79. *Provider of emergencies*

80. *Cupboard organizer*

81. *Freezer filler*

82. *Authority on Tupperware and other plastic containers*

83 *to* **88.** *All-around etiquette expert:*
sub-specialty in baby's manners

89. *Dispenser of platitudes*

90. *Dispenser of chicken soup*

91. *Dispenser of guilt*

92. *Interior decorator*

93. *Dietician and menu planner*
specializing in low-sodium diets

94. *Knowledgeable fruit shopper*

95. *Coupon clipper par excellence*

96. *Sale spotter*

97. *Experienced rectal thermometer inserter*

98. *TV critic,*
best at knowing what baby should *not* watch

99. *Real estate expert*

100. *Family planning consultant*

101. *Walking photo album*

BABY PROFILE # 83

The Brontosaurus

Birth weight: 12 lbs. and up
Duration of labor: 6 weeks
Favorite food: all of Carvel's special holiday cakes
Temperament: likes birthday parties
Favorite toy: Pound-a-Ball
Favorite TV personality: Willard Scott
Favorite activity: staring at sky; banging things until
they break
First word: "More"

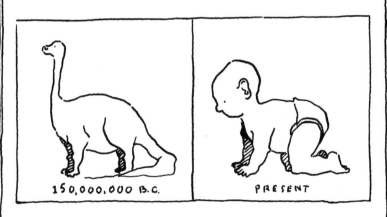

150,000,000 B.C.   PRESENT

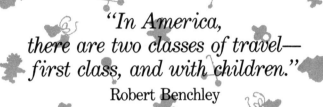

*"In America,
there are two classes of travel—
first class, and with children."*
Robert Benchley

*"The thing that impresses me
about America is the way parents obey
their children."*
Duke of Windsor

4

tHe Bigger worLd

The Old Lady on the Street Department

or

"ADVICE FROM THOSE WHO REALLY KNOW BEST, DEAR"

One of the biggest surprises for new parents is the phenomenon known as "The Old Lady on the Street." Long ignored by sociologists (partly because of their innocuous colorings), this fascinating sub-group assumes tremendous importance for the new Mom and Dad. Nearly invisible before the birth of baby, suddenly flocks of these ancient magistrates are encountered every-where—looking for the slightest violation in proper baby-care or etiquette. (Of course, they don't go out hoping to find neglected babies, it's just that they seem to crop up at every street crossing.) They are completely unrestrained in their criticism and "helpfulness," and new parents can find themselves answering to these self-appointed vigilantes several times a day.

For *your* protection, we have summarized the
major "Old Lady Obsessions." Arm
yourself with this knowledge! If you do get
caught, remember your best weapon
is a frozen smile and a blank stare. Engaging in
any conversation is an admission of guilt!

Strollers
"Be careful he doesn't fall out. You can't trust
those things. Is he strapped in?"

Pacifiers:
"Oh, don't get her started on that. It will be trouble
from now on."

Weight:
"Only twelve months old! Why, she is a little
fatty, isn't she?"

Bedtime:
"Isn't it too late for the poor little thing to be out?"

Food:
"Going home for a nice bowl of soup, sweetheart?"
"What, no soup?"

Hats:
"Isn't it too cold not to wear a hat?"

"Isn't it too windy not to wear a hat?"

"Isn't it too draughty not to wear a hat?"

"Isn't it too hot to wear a hat?"

Street Crossings:
"Watch the baby crossing the street. TAKE HER HAND!"

Gender:

As a public service, here is a listing
of high density/low density geriatric areas:

Intense Old Lady Hot Spots	Relatively Risk-free Areas
Park benches	Roller discos
Curb sides	Drive-in movies
Church sales	Jazz clubs
Bingo halls	Circus sideshows
Lottery offices	Drag racetracks
Bus terminals	Christopher Street
Supermarkets	Hot tub showrooms
Post Offices	Swingers' clubs
Yarn stores	"Certain" movies
Drug stores	Lamaze classes
Playgrounds	Any Club Med
Department store ladies rooms	Pool Halls
Anywhere dry and warm	Methadone clinics

WARNING: Not all "Old Ladies on the Street" are of the female gender, or old. There are several "Honorary Old Lady" types. Beware of the following:

Any old man carrying three or more shopping bags and heading toward you.

Any old-maidish woman who talks to baby exclusively and gives you the evil eye.

Packs of young girls age 8 to 13.

"The Toughest Baby Trivia Test in the World"

Attention trivia fans and those aspiring to perfect parenthood—
How good a parent do you think you are? Can you stand up to the best? We all know about dressing, feeding, bonding, and other essentials of raising baby... but what about those little extras that only a *SUPER PARENT* would know? Are you ready to be tested? See how you rate against the real pros:

---

1. According to *The First Twelve Months of Life,* in what month will babies first do the following:

a. sleep all night

b. throw temper tantrums

c. experience separation anxiety

2. How many medium-size Luvs are there in the convenience pack?

3. Tri-Vi-Sol contains three vitamins. Name them.

4. Besides Kermit the Frog, name two people who have sung "It Ain't Easy Being Green."

5. How many servings are there in a container of Yoplait yogurt?

6. What are the three foods most often prescribed to combat baby's diarrhea?

7. Give the **full** name of the most over-publicized new baby of 1982.

8. Where do Prince Tuesday and King Friday live?

9. In *The Telephone Book* by Dorothy Kunhardt, to whom is the letter Timmy is allowed to take out of Mommy's pocketbook addressed?

10. Name one gourmet cheese that reminds you of dirty diapers.

11. Bert of *Sesame Street*'s Bert and Ernie has a twin brother. What is his name?

12. Name the title of one adult book.

13. Give three original excuses why your mother-in-law can't come over on Sunday.

14. Besides collecting dust, name three things a potty chair can be used for.

15. What time does the *Six O'Clock News* come on?

16. Which is the most painful:

    a. broken leg

    b. watching Jerry Lewis movies

    c. childbirth

17. Who said, "I wanted a creature only a mother could love?"

BONUS QUESTION

Match these famous parents to their offspring:

Polar bear at Bronx Zoo	Fernando Valenzuela Jr.
Gepetto the Shoemaker	Bo Derek
Fernando Valenzuela	Sno Cap
John Derek	Pinocchio
"Baby Doc" Duvalier	Spot the Dog
Daddy Fry-Baby	Baby Fry-Baby
Sally the Dog	Baby, "Baby Doc" Duvalier

ANSWERS:
Score one point for each correct answer. Bonus points given for "extra-tough" questions

1. a. third month
   b. twelfth
   c. every month.

2. 48.

3. A, D, and C.

4. Frank Sinatra, Van Morrison. BONUS! SCORE 3 EXTRA POINTS!

5. 2 adult, or 1 baby.

6. Bananas, applesauce, and rice cereal.

7. Prince William Arthur Phillip Louis Windsor, heir to the British throne. (Score only for full name).

8. In *Mister Rogers' Neighborhood, Land of Make-Believe.*

9. Mr. E. Johnson
654 North Street
Brooklyn, N.Y. 10037
BONUS! SCORE
5 EXTRA POINTS!!!

10. Pont L'Evêque, Maroilles, Taleggio. Deduct two points if you said any American, or processed cheese.

11. Bart.

12. *War and Peace.* Score 10 extra points if you've read more than one page from any book without pictures during the last six months.

13. Score 5 points if you said any of the below:

   a. you have an appointment with counselor from local sex therapy clinic

   b. you're helping neighbors take their in-laws to see a nursing home

   c. you're hoping to have a hangover. (Deduct 5 points for any excuse involving illness, food, sleep, or husband's mood.)

14. 1. climbing into bathtub

   2. storing toys

   3. ice-bucket.

15. 6 pm. Score 2 points if you didn't sneak a look at *TV Guide.*

16. Any Jerry Lewis movie made after 1957.

17. Steven Spielberg about E.T.

RATING

42 or more: *Wow!* You're really into this. Don't you have anything else to do?

Over 30: You're still way up there. Good babysitting material.

Over 20: A good try.

10 to 20: Recommend subscribing to *Parents* magazine.

Under 5: Suggest you find a guardian for baby quickly.

BABY PROFILE # 63

The Perfect Baby

(other people's babies)

Birth weight: 7 lbs., on the nose
Duration of labor: 30 minutes
Favorite food: anything mom cooks
Temperament: similar to processed cheese
Favorite toy: *Family Circle* magazine
Means of transportation: walks in a straight line
Relationship with parents: one of love, loyalty, and obedience
First word: "Please"

New Mother's Domestic Self-defense Techniques

"free again..."

#1. The Difficult Mother-in-Law

Mother-in-law can be an enormous help. In fact,
sometimes she can be too helpful.
In the daily life of the average harassed mother,
there may be many occasions when
she becomes "too much." At these times,
you need some ways to persuade
her to leave matters in your capable hands (or to
leave entirely). If you ever find
this happening to you, herewith are:

9 Easy Ways of Communicating with a Difficult Mother-in-Law

1. Casually mention that the baby called *your*
   mother "Grandma" all weekend.

2. Get an unlisted phone number.

3. If she offers to help, show her the laundry room.

4. Mention that "for personal reasons" you may have to move 500 miles away.

5. When she shows baby off to her friends, remark that baby looks like everybody else but her.

6. Tell her not to bother to cook for baby because he/she has sophisticated tastes.

7. Tell her how much baby reminds you of her family, especially at mealtimes.

8. Let her know you are thinking of spending baby's first birthday with *your* parents.

9. Casually ask her if she knows anyone who has had a vasectomy.

#2. The Noisy Neighbors

cont. on Page 204

****
"Behind every successful parent stands a
surprised mother-in-law."
with thanks to Hubert Humphrey
****

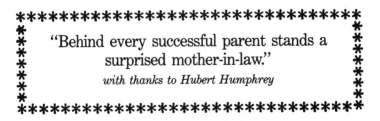

THE *NO BAD BABIES*tm BOARD GAME

Get Baby into the Right Nursery School

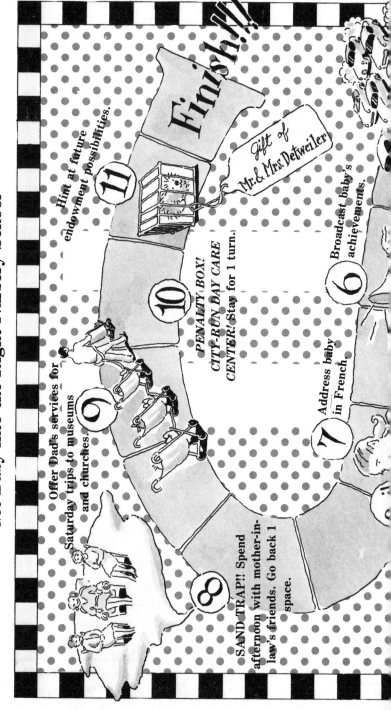

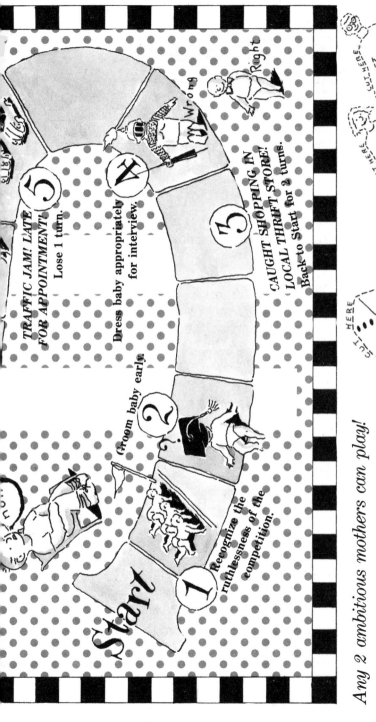

TRAFFIC JAM! LATE FOR APPOINTMENT! Lose 1 turn.

Dress baby appropriately for interview.

Wrong · Right

CAUGHT SHOPPING IN LOCAL THRIFT STORE! Back to Start for 2 turns.

Groom baby early.

Recognize the ruthlessness of the competition.

Start

Any 2 ambitious mothers can play!

Object: Get your baby into nursery school first!

To Play: Throw 1 die. Advance as indicated. Must have *exact* number to finish.

CUT HERE · CUT HERE · CUT HERE · CUT HERE · CUT HERE

Terrible Babies in History (Rated 1 to 5)

Some people are born terrible babies.
Some become them along the way. Still others
develop into terrible babies after many
years. In any case, if you're a new mother or
father and you think you've got it
bad, think about what life must have been like for
the parents of the following:

1
Bored Even Grandmother

Heidi

Shirley Temple

Sigmund Freud

Yoko Ono

All of the Osmonds

John Davidson

Sandy Duncan

Dr. Joyce Brothers

Steve Garvey

Rod McKuen

Snoopy

Kathy "Kitten" Anderson

Clark Kent

2
Stole Other Babies' Toys

Mean Joe Green

Harry Houdini

Rosie Ruiz

Al Capone

Suzanne Somers

3
Never Stopped Whining

Elizabeth Taylor

All of the Fondas

Sen. Joseph McCarthy

Patty Duke Astin

John McEnroe

Grace Slick

4
Takes After In-Laws

J. R. Ewing

Virginia Graham

Howard Cosell

5
Beyond the Pale

Florence Henderson

Adolph Hitler

Idi Amin

Marquis de Sade

Genghis Khan

The Ayatollah Khomeini

Count Dracula

Evita

Lizzie Borden

Special Awards go to:
Must Take After Step-Mother

Christina Onassis

Still Babies

Annette Funicello

Pia Zadora

Cheryl Tiegs

Dick Clark

Princess Diana

Became Babies

Howard Hughes

Jerry Lewis

Orson Welles

Allan Carr

Elvis Presley

Was Never a Baby

Adrian Arpel

Rosemary Rogers

James Watt

Paloma Picasso

John Houseman

Helen Hayes

Babies We Wish We Had Known

Ralph & Alice Kramden

Mel Brooks

Albert Brooks

Morris the Cat

Bob Elliot

Ray Goulding

Georgia O'Keeffe

Alice Roosevelt Longworth

Richard Pryor

Ethel Mertz

Our husbands

How to Avoid the 10 Most Embarrassing Public Occasions with Baby

Babies are known for their unpredictability.
Spontaneous, fun-loving creatures,
they seem to have an infallible knack for doing
those things that parents most
dread. To prepare new mothers and fathers
for these inevitable situations, *No
Bad Babies* has compiled a list of popular
baby-caused social disasters, along
with suggestions for coping.

1. BABY vomits on spouse's
   boss at Christmas party.

You could:
a. Act as if nothing unusual had happened.
b. Start a chorus of "For He's a Jolly Good Fellow."
c. Fix yourself a strong drink.

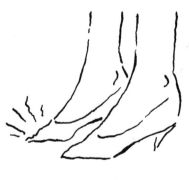

2. BABY passes gas loudly during sister-in-law's wedding.

You could:
a. Look angrily at groom.
b. Look angrily at husband.
c. Hand baby to mother-in-law.

3. BABY spills entire meal on floor in expensive restaurant.

You could:
a. Excuse yourself to make important phone call.
b. Make joke about how baby is just like in-laws.
c. Send back the wine.

4. BABY throws loud tantrum during long airplane ride.

You could:
a. Say in loud voice, "Your mother will be back soon, darling."
b. Commandeer drinks trolley.
c. Store baby in overhead compartment.

5. BABY urinates on Grandma and Grandpa in front of their guests.

You could:
a. Remind them they always wanted a grandchild.
b. Tell them the stain will wash out.
c. Ask if anyone has a camera.

6. BABY persists in making "raspberry" noises during church service.

You could:
a. Raise your eyes upward.
b. Sleep late next Sunday.
c. Go to a Gospel church in future.

7. BABY has diarrhea in crowded department store.

You could:
a. Burst into tears.
b. Ask anyone who looks disgusted to get you paper towels.
c. Buy yourself something expensive before leaving.

8. BABY cries uncontrollably during movie husband desperately wanted to see.

You could:
a. Slip away to ladies room and try to watch movie from there.
b. Ask if there is a pediatrician in the house.
c. Give baby Ju-Jubes to induce lockjaw.

9. BABY pulls other baby's hair at playground and refuses to let go.

You could:
a. Ask the mother if she wants to start playgroup at her house.
b. Remark on how the "rough" neighborhood is affecting your child.
c. Suggest to mother that her baby could use haircut.

10. BABY breaks rare crystal vase at friend's house.

You could:
a. Observe how ephemeral the beautiful things in life are.
b. Volunteer to do the dishes.
c. Say that you've lost three that way already.

****
* "Two of anything but children make a pair. *
*   Two of them make a mob."   *
*   *Reflections of a Bachelor*   *
****

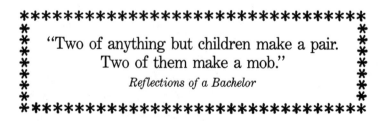

BABY PROFILE # 11

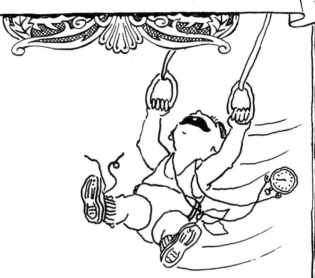

The Athletic Baby

Birth weight: 8 lbs. 4 ozs.
Duration of labor: 2 hours, 31 minutes, 2.4 secs.
Temperament: limitless indifference to tedium
Favorite Toy: Fisher-Price Play Gym
Means of transportation: Nike's
Favorite TV personality: Magic Johnson
First word: "Tendon"

Parents Bill of Rights... and other lost causes

— Parents shall have the right to be informed about the risks, hazards, and side-effects of attending any one-year old's birthday party

— Mother shall have the right to refuse to pose for any photos or videotape.

— Spouses shall have the right to be informed of any weekend-long visits from in-laws... before they arrive.

— Parents shall have the right to limit reading PAT THE BUNNY to no more than twelve times a day.

— Parents shall have the right to complain endlessly about how hard things are now.

— Father shall have the right to expect a foot-wide pathway through baby's toys on floor... providing he clears it.

— Mother shall have the right not to listen to father's imitations of Kermit the Frog, Bert and Ernie and the Count.

— Parents shall have the right to eat dinner together... at least once every two months.

— Mother shall have the right to insist that Dad take his Mother's phone calls.

— Parents shall have the right to think that their baby is the only good-looking one in the playground.

— Parents shall have the right not to go to Toys-R-Us™ during the months of November and December.

— Parents shall have the right to expect normal sexual activity... in four or five years.

— Mother shall have the right to sleep late... on April 1, 1989.

— Parents shall have the right to take a screaming baby into bed with them

Glossary

Abdomen
Part of Mom's body that will never look the same again.

Airplane Travel
Test of parental *chutzpah*.

Allergy
Condition developed by new fathers to dirty diapers.

Baby Boom
Sound made by angry baby.

Baby Sitter
The only person who gets paid for watching baby.

Bedtime
Ritual one-sided contest between flagging parents and determined baby.

Circumcision
First lesson young male gets in the art of leaving "good tips."

Colic
Baby's classic way of testing your marriage.

Creative Activities
Watching Mr. Rogers put on sneakers.

Diaper Rash
Incidence following diet of prunes and juice.

Enema
Procedure probably inspired by the Marquis de

Sade for use in childbirth.

Episiotomy
Favorite joke of obstetrician – it will keep Mom in stitches for weeks!

False Labor
Not the real thing, but hurts like the real thing.

Finger Foods
Projectiles.

Guilt
See Mother-in-Law.

Hospital Rest
One of the "Three Biggest Lies" about childbirth. See *Parents' sleeptime* and *Sexual activity* for the other two.

Let-Down Reflex
How Mom's body feels at the end of the day; how Dad's feels after sex.

Meconium
Reputedly the world's worst bowel movement; unforgiveable form of verbal abuse.

Mother-in-Law
See *Guilt*.

Nap
Weekend afternoon activity of baby and Dad.

Nursing Bra
See the La Leche League's brilliant satire: *NOT The Frederick's of Hollywood Catalog.*

Pacifier
Invention created to save expensive child therapy sessions.

Quality Time
Concept originated in late-20th century California. See chapter on "Guilt" for full explanation.

Security Blanket
Trust fund of over $100,000 for Mom's use.

Self-Help Routines
What your mother-in-law remembers instilling in her child at an early age.

Sexual Intercourse
Activity allegedly engaged in by childless couples.

Sleep
Activity allegedly engaged in by childless couples.

Soranus
Ancient Roman gynecologist (130 AD) after whom this condition is named.

Tantrums
Baby's version of primal scream.

Television
Invention created to save expensive parent therapy sessions.

Whining
Form of behavior passed down through Y chromosome.

Working Parents
Situation in which *both* parents are paid for their labors.

BABY PROFILE # 5023

Baby of the Future

Birth weight: 2.5 kilos
Length of labor: 13 seconds
Favorite food: bananas and Tang
Love object: great-grandmother's old E.T. doll
Temperament: groks everything
Means of transportation: nuclear-powered Perego stroller
Preferred reading: *Pat the Robot*
Favorite activity: cloning neighbor's toys
Favorite TV personality: Mr. Rogers
Bedtime: Earth time 21.00 hours;
Mars time 12.5.6

Sincere thanks to:

John Smallwood

our husbands,
Peter Van Raalte
and Mark Levine

Judy & Leo Linkiewicz

And to all our
friends and neighbors who
tried to get into
this book.